PEOPLE IN THE PAST

Ancient Greek Children

Richard Tames

Heinemann Library
Chicago, Illinois

Customer Service 888-454-2279
Visit our website at www.heinemannlibrary.com

Text and cover designed by Tinstar
Originated by Ambassador Litho
Printed by Wing King Tong in Hong Kong
07 06 05 04 03
10 9 8 7 6 5 4 3 2 1

Library of Congress Cataloging-in-Publication Data
Tames, Richard.
  Ancient Greek Children / Richard Tames.
      p. cm. -- (People in the past)
Includes bibliographical references and index.
  ISBN 1-58810-639-X (HC) 1-4034-0131-4 (Pbk)
  1. Children--Greece--History--Juvenile literature. 2.
Children--Greece--Social life and customs--Juvenile literature. 3.
Children--Greece--Social conditions--Juvenile literature. 4.
Greece--Civilization--To 146 B.C.--Juvenile literature. [1.
Greece--Civilization--To 146 B.C.] I. Title. II. Series.
  HQ792.G73 T36 2002
  305.23'09495--dc21
                              2001007491

Acknowledgments
The author and publishers are grateful to the following for permission to reproduce copyright material: Ancient Art and Architecture Collection, pp. 6, 7, 10, 14, 16, 18, 31, 33, 34; AKG London, pp. 8, 12, 21, 22, 24, 26, 30, 32, 36, 40, 41; Werner Forman Archive, pp. 11, 42; Bridgeman Art Library, p. 25; Michael Holford, p. 28; British Museum, p. 38; Richard Butler and Magnet Harlequin, p. 43.
Cover photograph reproduced with permission of Ancient Art and Architecture Collection.

Some words are shown in bold, **like this.** You can find out what they mean by looking in the glossary.

Contents

The World of the Ancient Greeks

◄► ◄► ◄► ◄► ◄► ◄► ◄► ◄► ◄► ◄► ◄► ◄► ◄► ◄► ◄► ◄► ◄►

When people talk about ancient Greece, they do not just mean the modern-day country of Greece as it used to be. The ancient Greek world was made up of the hot, rocky mainland of Greece and hundreds of islands in the Aegean, Ionian, and Adriatic Seas, as well as settlements overseas, in places ranging from northern Africa to what we now call Turkey and Italy. The earliest Greek speakers did not think that they all belonged to a single country. For a long time, they did not even think that they all belonged to the same **civilization.**

For centuries, the mightiest people in the Greek world were the Minoans, based on the island of Crete. Power then passed to the warlike Mycenaeans, based on the mainland, in the region known as the **Peloponnese.** This was followed, around 1100 B.C.E., by centuries of confusion and upheaval. Later, in the Classical Age, from about 500 B.C.E. until about 300 B.C.E., prosperity was restored by the rise of many city-states, such as Athens and Sparta. The Greek word for city-state is **polis.** Each *polis* controlled the villages and farmland around it.

What we owe the Greeks

We look back to ancient Greece as the origin of the Western civilization that has evolved in Europe, North America, and elsewhere. Greeks invented **democracy,** drama, and trial by jury. The Greeks were curious and were willing to learn from the **Babylonians** and the Egyptians. After Greece became part of the Roman Empire, the Romans valued the Greek language and Greek learning, and passed them on to future generations.

Forming our language

Thousands of Greek words have passed into other European languages. Automatic, cycle, **martyr,** museum, police, and politics are all Greek words. Many modern words are based on Greek words. For example, "technology" comes from the Greek words *techne,* meaning craft or know how, and *logos,* meaning word or science.

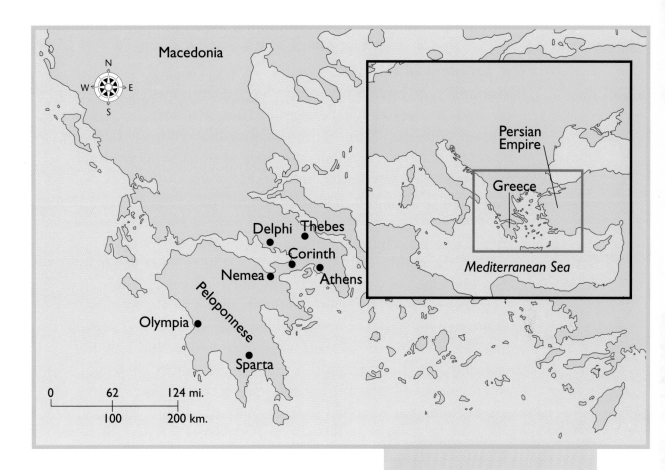

This book is about children in ancient Greece, so it is about becoming a Greek and everything that meant: learning the language, customs, and beliefs handed on from one generation to the next. Nowadays it is often said that "our children are the future." The ancient Greeks had tremendous confidence in the Greek way of life, but in their world they cannot have been so confident about the survival of their own family. Greeks often died young, either from untreatable diseases or in wars between the city-states. This meant that attitudes to childhood were often very different from those we know today.

Ancient Greece was not a single, unified country but was instead a collection of many separate states that often waged war on one another. The ancient Greeks used the word *Hellas* to describe all the places where there was a Greek way of life.

Invisible children

The problem of the past

Historians try to build a picture of the past from the things people made and the documents they wrote. These two sorts of evidence help each other out. Most of the evidence that we have, however, is based on either things made by adults or documents written by adults. So it can often be difficult to find out about the lives of children who lived more than 2,000 years ago.

The Parthenon is a **temple** in Athens **dedicated** to the city's **guardian,** the goddess Athena. Athena was just one of the many gods and goddesses worshiped by the ancient Greeks. There is a carved **frieze** around the Parthenon that shows girls presenting a new dress to the goddess. From written sources, we also know that young girls wove the dress. This helps us to understand how the Greeks thought about girlhood. Young girls were thought to be pure and innocent, possibly because Greek society was run by men, meaning that boys had to worry about less pure things, such as war and money. Because of this, girls were also thought to be best fitted to **weave** a dress for a goddess and to present it to her in person on behalf of the whole community.

Making things

Examples like the Parthenon frieze are rather unusual. Children growing up in ancient Greece often helped adults to build houses or to make pottery as they learned these trades from their elders. The resulting products, however, were still essentially designed and made by adults. The child's contribution—fetching tools or helping to mix clay—remains invisible.

This vase gives information about adult life, but a child may have been involved in making it.

We cannot, therefore, learn much about ancient Greek children from what they made or helped to make. We can learn something from what was made for them, such as toys, and from what was made about them, such as paintings or carvings showing children.

Words

Only a minority of Greek children learned to read and write. Examples of how and what we suppose they learned have survived. Yet children did not write about themselves. When they were old enough to do so, they were no longer children.

Thinking about childhood

Although some important Greek thinkers, such as Plato and Aristotle, did write about children, they wrote mainly about how children ought to be brought up, not how they actually were brought up. It is possible that Plato and Aristotle had no children of their own. Plato did, however, realize that how children learned to play could have a powerful effect on the formation of their character as adults.

Women were closest to children because they spent much more time with them than men did. Greek homes were divided into areas for men and areas for women. Until they were about six years old, boys and girls both spent nearly all their time in the women's quarters of a Greek home.

This huge Greek theater—and Greek drama in general—was intended for adults only.

Babies

Danger and delight

Childbirth in ancient Greece was very risky. Wives were expected to have one baby after another. A wife unable to bear children was pitied by other women, who thought she was cursed by the gods. Women who could not have children were likely to live longer than the women who pitied them. Many women died giving birth. Repeated childbirth weakened mothers and increased the danger of later births. About half of all women died by the age of 40 years. Because husbands were usually much older than wives, few men lived to see their grandchildren grow up.

When a healthy baby was born, there was a celebration. Relatives gathered at the house to see the new child.

This statue from about 375 B.C.E. shows an old nurse with a baby. Only wealthy families could afford nurses to look after their children. In poorer homes, the mother took care of the baby herself.

The father carried a new baby around the house. Friends and family sent gifts. The doorway of the home was decorated with a **wreath** of olives for a boy, or a wreath of wool for a girl. Greek families wanted boys, not girls. A boy would **inherit** family property, carry on the family name, and become a warrior for his *polis.* A girl had to be married, and that usually meant payment of a **dowry.**

To live or to die

A new baby was anxiously examined for defects. A loud cry was taken as a sign of a very healthy baby. Sick or deformed children, especially girls, were often left outside to die. A child with a crooked limb or even red hair might be thought to show that the gods were angry for some reason. Such a child might be a burden on the family and might give birth to other damaged children. Children who were not 100-percent healthy were not always thrown away, especially if they were boys.

Names

Greek children were given only one name. This might refer to a god or goddess (Herodotus, meaning given by Hera), an animal (Philippos or Philip, meaning lover of horses), or a plant (Phyllis, meaning a green bough). Some names reflected family pride: Cleopatra means "glory of her father," and Demosthenes means "the people's strength." In public a person may also have been called by either his father's name ("son of …") or the village from which he came. The first male child was often named after his father's father, the second after his mother's father, the third after one of his father's uncles, and so on. Any nickname that a person was given as an adult remained personal and was not handed on to children.

Caring for Children

The ancient Greeks did not think of babies as cute little angels who should be marveled at, fussed over, and spoiled with gifts and treats. A baby was everything that an adult man should not be. It was physically weak, stupid, easily fooled, and without either memory or self-control. Good qualities had to be instilled into the baby by its upbringing to make it into a satisfactory adult. A satisfactory man could both fight to defend his city and take part in running it. Satisfactory women were expected to be obedient, to be able both to run a house, and to be able to raise children of their own.

Myths of childhood

Some favorite Greek **myths** told stories about extraordinary babies whose amazing deeds showed that they would one day become heroes. One myth said that when the hero Hercules was born, the goddess Hera sent snakes to kill him in his cradle. The baby Hercules survived by strangling the snakes. This story was told to show that Hercules had enormous strength, even as a baby. In another myth, the warrior Achilles killed a wild boar when he was only six years old. Alexander the Great, who was a real person, was supposed to have tamed a horse while he was only a boy.

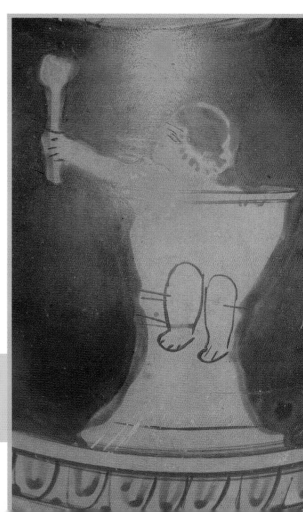

This kind of clay pot kept a baby from wandering around in the house, and served as a toilet at the same time.

The popularity of these stories shows the Greeks believed that tough fighters, whether they were gods or humans, were once tough children. The Athenian politician Hyperides said, "We educate children so that they may become good men and they show that they were well educated as children by being especially brave in battle."

Method

The **philosopher** Plato described good Greek child care. Because babies had soft skin and flexible bones, the Greeks wrapped babies up tightly until they were two years old, to make their joints grow strong and their limbs grow straight. They carried children around until they were three years old, rather than making them walk too early. Nowadays, toddlers are encouraged to walk as soon as possible.

Plato said that when Greek children did walk they should go barefoot, to toughen their feet. From three until six years of age, they should play with other children. By the age of seven years, when their baby teeth had fallen out and had been replaced by adult teeth, they should be ready to begin their education, and boys should then be separated from girls.

Greek children usually grew up in large households where aunts, female slaves, and older sisters, as well as their own mothers, helped to bring them up. This carving shows a Greek child with its female caregivers.

Home Comforts

Keep it simple

Most Greek homes were one-story houses made of sunbaked mud bricks, with thick walls, small, shuttered windows, and an open, airy **courtyard** in the center, surrounded by bedrooms, storerooms, and the kitchen. The grandest room was a dining room used for male guests or family **ceremonies.** Children would normally be kept from this room. Even wealthy homes had only wooden-framed beds, couches, stools, and chests for storage. Country houses were often larger because land was cheaper in the country.

Courtyard life

The courtyard was the focus of family life and was where girls and women spent most of their time. It let light and air into rooms that would otherwise be cool and dark. Cooking on portable **hearths** or **braziers** could be done outside in warm weather, which was much more pleasant than cooking in a hot, smoke-filled kitchen. Small children could play safely in the courtyard with their friends or animals. There was also room to do messy jobs, such as washing sheep's fleece.

Here, a boy calls to his dog. Dogs would have been used to guard homes at night and to protect sheep from wolves.

Greek houses were divided into different areas for men and women. Children were usually looked after by their mothers so, naturally, they spent most of their time in the female part of the house, as well as in the courtyard. Men often entertained guests in their part of the house and it would have been a big step in a young man's life when he was invited to these parties. Girls would move to the house of their husband when they married.

Daily bread

The Greeks divided food into two sorts, *sitos* and *opson*. *Sitos* was bread, biscuit, cake, or hot cereal. This was made from either wheat or barley, and often had beans, peas, or lentils mixed into it. *Sitos* was supposed to be filling. *Opson* was whatever topping was put on top of *sitos*, such as olive oil or salt. Fish and shellfish, rather than meat, provided **protein** in the Greek diet. Meat was only eaten after being **sacrificed** to the gods. It was a special treat for special days. Children rarely ate it.

Fresh bread or hot cereal was made daily, so grinding wheat or barley into flour was a regular chore for girls. Milk was used for cheese, rather than as a drink. Girls regularly helped their mothers with baking, milking, cheese making, and pressing olives for their oil. They also gathered nuts, berries, and honey, which was the only sweetener.

Did the Greeks keep pets?

Greek children came into contact with animals, particularly if they lived in the country, but they would probably not understand modern attitudes toward pets. Although there are pictures that show children playing with dogs, these animals would have had a practical use. In the city, dogs guarded the house. In the countryside, men used dogs to hunt for food.

Clothes and Fashions

The weather in Greece is normally warm and dry, although some of the mountainous areas can be cold in winter. The clothes that most ancient Greek children wore did not need to be too warm because the weather was often hot.

Materials

Both cloth and clothes were made at home by the mother of the family, helped by her daughters and slaves. This was true of the rich as well as of ordinary families. The main materials were wool and linen. Girls first learned to spin wool into yarn. Then they learned to **weave** yarn into cloth on a loom, to make clothes, blankets, cushions, and wall hangings.

This carving shows the long, flowing lines typical of Greek clothing.

Making linen was a long business, but each stage was simple enough for children to help with. **Flax** plants were gathered by hand, tied in bundles, dried out, combed to remove seeds, and soaked in water to separate the fibers. The fibers were beaten to soften them, and then were washed and spun into yarn to be woven. In fine linen, the flax fibers were thinner and less rough. Coarse linen was used for bags or aprons, and fine linen was used for things that, like underwear or **tunics,** needed to be smoother because they were worn next to the skin. Most materials were undyed. Richer people wore clothes that were colored with dyes that were made from plants.

Finding out about clothes

Although no clothes have survived from the time, most of what we know about Greek children's clothing comes from writings and paintings on vases. Often, though, Greeks were shown naked on vases, to distinguish them from foreigners, who are shown wearing clothes. This makes it even more difficult to find out what Greek children wore. Statues tell us a lot about clothing and hairstyles, but they cannot usually tell us about the colors of clothes. On those statues that were painted, in most cases, the paint wore off long ago.

Garments

There was little difference between the clothes worn by males and females, and little difference in the clothes worn by adults and children. Styles changed little over centuries. Mothers and daughters wore ankle-length loose dresses, which were belted at the waist and pinned at the shoulder. Girls wore white until they were married. Boys wore knee-length tunics, and men wore longer tunics. In cold weather, cloaks or shawls were worn. In Sparta, where the army was all-important, boys wore only a thin cloak and went barefoot year round to toughen them up.

Leather sandals were the most common footwear in Greece. People who lived in the country often went barefoot. Both girls and boys let their hair grow long but often braided it to keep it out of the way.

Family Life

Sharing the house

The Greeks had no word for family in the common modern sense. Instead they referred to the group of related people who lived together as an **oikos,** or what we would call a household. A Greek household included not only a married couple and their children but also their slaves, animals, land, house, buildings, and sometimes their relatives, such as grandparents and unmarried female relatives. In big cities, the *oikos* might also include strangers who rented rooms. Everyone in the *oikos* obeyed the male head of the household.

In this farewell scene, a mother (seated) says good-bye to her daughter. Girls would leave the family home to be married.

Tribes and brotherhoods

Athens, like many city-states, began as a society made up of tribes; each led by a warrior chief. To remind Athenians of their past, they kept these tribes as an important part of society. Each household belonged to one of the tribes, called **phylae**. Each tribe was made up of brotherhoods, **phratrai**, headed by an aristocratic family. Each family was a member of one of the *phratrai*. A young boy was presented publicly to his *phratry* by his father and uncles, knowing that when he grew up and headed a household of his own he could look to its members for support in disputes or times of trouble.

A big, happy family

Greeks liked large families. Family members could help each other in work and politics, so the bigger a family, the richer and more powerful it could become. The more children that parents had, the better chance there would be that some would survive to look after their parents in their advanced age. When a married couple either failed to have children of their own or lost their children through illness or accident, they often adopted others so that there would be someone to **inherit** their property, to carry on the family name, and to care for their tomb after they died. Fathers who only had daughters might adopt one of their son-in-laws, because a daughter could not inherit the family property.

Family changes

The mother's job was to have children, to bring them up, and to organize the household. Girls married in their early teens, often to men who were twenty years older. As a result of repeated childbirth, many wives died in their twenties or thirties. As a result, husbands might remarry two or three times. This meant that many children were brought up by stepmothers and, among the rich, by nurses. If her husband died, a woman usually took the children to live with a male relative. If she was still young, then she would be encouraged to remarry.

Sparta Was Different

A soldier society

Sparta was different from every other Greek city-state because it was organized for war as a way of life. All ordinary work in Sparta was done by slaves called *helots*. Spartan men were the only full-time army in ancient Greece. Spartan boys grew up knowing that their future was to be a soldier.

Fit to live?

Every male child was inspected at birth to see if he was fit to live. A panel of older men, not the baby's father, made the decision. Sick or deformed babies were left outside to die of starvation or cold. Spartan mothers washed their babies in wine, not water, because they believed this would strengthen their babies.

Training for war

At seven years of age, boys left their family to live in **barracks.** They learned a little reading and writing, but most of their time was spent on gymnastics, athletics, and rough team games that were led by older boys. They also learned marching songs and a special kind of dancing, as a preparation for military **drills.** From twelve years of age onward, their training got even harder.

This Spartan soldier from the 6th century B.C.E. wears a crested helmet to make him look taller. Boys would have to get used to wearing such a helmet, which protected the cheeks and nose. Also, soldiers wore close-fitting armor to protect their chest and lower legs.

Boys were deliberately kept short of food so that they would learn to endure hunger and so that they would practice stealing food. Although this was a useful skill in wartime, being caught stealing led to a savage beating. Weapons training focused on the handling of the **infantry's** 9 $^2/_3$-foot (3-meter) spear and heavy bronze shield. Spartans thought that **cavalry** was for weaklings and that **archery** was for cowards.

Grown up

Spartan boys spent their last teenage year training younger boys. At twenty years of age, they were allowed to grow long hair and were elected to a **mess** of about fifteen men. They would eat and live with this group. From 30 years of age onward, they were allowed to have a say in politics. By 30 years of age, they should have married and begun to have children but they would remain with their mess, not their wife, until they were more than 60 years old.

Tough girls

Spartan girls had to learn to be tough, just as the boys did. We know that Spartan girls trained as athletes. In other city-states, athletics was mostly for men. Girls were taught how to run a household on their own, because when they married, their husbands would be gone for so much of the time.

Treatment of toddlers

Plutarch, a Roman who wrote in the 1st and 2nd centuries C.E., described how infants were brought up in Sparta:

"They were not closely wrapped up but grew freely ... ate whatever they were given; were not afraid of the dark or being left alone; and were not allowed tantrums or sulking or crying. For this reason Spartan nurses were often ... hired by people of other countries ..."

The World of Work

Perhaps because so much hard and heavy work was done by slaves, the Greeks did not respect it. Instead they admired men with leisure time for education, poetry, sports, and politics. Wealthy Greeks thought that craftsmen were little better than the slaves with whom the craftsmen worked. The wealthy Greeks did, however, admire the wonderful skills that craftsmen possessed.

Helping at home

Children, especially in poor families, who often did not have slaves, were expected to help out at home. Regular jobs included looking after younger children, gathering **fodder** and fuel, and clearing stones from fields and throwing them at birds to protect the crops. Because Greece has little good **grazing land,** it was more common to keep goats and sheep than cows. Because goats are much smaller than cows, it was easier to put boys in charge of their herding. In the autumn, boys would climb the olive trees to shake the ripe olives to the ground.

Water was needed for washing and cooking, as well as drinking, so fetching it from a river, well, or fountain was done several times a day. Boys were usually sent on errands or used as messengers. Girls might look after the hens, which stayed close to the house. Most girls learned from their mother how to cook, to clean, to **weave** cloth, to nurse family members when they were sick, and generally to keep a home. Even girls in wealthy families were expected to do this, to show they were respectable and could supervise slaves—making sure that they were doing household tasks properly.

Defending the city

When fathers went away to war, older boys were expected to take charge of the slaves left behind and make sure that they still did their work properly. In a city under attack, boys were expected to support its defenders by passing **ammunition**, such as arrows and stones for slings and **catapults,** to the fighting front. Boys were also expected to help by rebuilding damaged walls.

Do it like Dad

Many boys did not go to school, but were brought up to do whatever jobs their father did, learning the trade from him. Farmers' sons became farmers; craftsmen's' sons became craftsmen. Most businesses were small workshops, in which a man worked with his sons and one or two slaves, almost never more than ten people in all. The largest business ever recorded in ancient Greece had 120 employees making shields, but all of these workers were slaves.

Girls would stay at home and learn how to run a home. Some also learned the art of Greek dancing, illustrated in this statue.

Slavery

Slavery was common throughout the Greek world, particularly in Athens. A free Athenian without even one slave was thought to be poor.

Where did slaves come from?

Slavery was an alternative to killing captured prisoners of war. Often, the men of a conquered city would be killed, and the women and children would be sold off to traders, who followed armies around just to buy prisoners. Prisoners were sold to pay for the huge costs of war, which the **citizens** often had to pay themselves. Other slaves were bought from pirates who had kidnapped them. Children and teenagers were most in demand because they were easier to control and train and had a lifetime of work in them. Free adults were sometimes temporarily enslaved until they could pay off a debt. If they could not pay, their children could become slaves, too. Some slaves were babies that had been abandoned at birth. Anyone rescuing such a baby could bring it up as a slave. Most slaves were simply born as children of slaves.

This painting shows a slave using a yoke to carry large jars. Jars like these might have been used to store wine or olive oil.

How were slaves treated?

A small number of slaves were owned by governments and worked as police officers, clerks, porters, and messengers. Most slaves, especially child slaves, worked in households, helping with daily chores such as cleaning, washing, and cooking. Very bright slave children might be taught to read and write. Although household slaves could be beaten, it was not in their owner's interest to treat them harshly. Unhappy and unhealthy slaves worked badly. They might also damage things and even poison their owners. In very rich families, slaves were often given positions of trust as **physicians,** teachers, bookkeepers, or bodyguards. Some Greeks disapproved of letting slaves get too involved in bringing up their children. Because most slaves were not Greek, the child might learn foreign ideas and pick up bad manners or ways of speaking.

The lives of children of slaves depended greatly on their parents' good behavior. An owner could always sell slaves' children to another household as punishment for disobedience. Just the knowledge that the owner could do this was usually enough to keep their obedience.

Freedom

Some slaves were allowed to run their own businesses and to use the money they made to buy their freedom. In Athens, these freed men had the same limited rights as foreign residents did, but their children had the same full rights as citizens did, such as owning property and voting in elections.

Hard labor

Slaves were also used to mass-produce weapons and household goods such as pottery, beds, and knives. More than 30,000 slaves worked in the silver mines owned by the Athenian government. Many of these slaves were children, who were small enough to crawl into and work in narrow tunnels. They were treated very badly because they were not part of a household and because it was not in their masters' interests to treat them well. There were many accidents in the mine, and many slaves were hurt or killed in the accidents.

Education

Private fee-paying schools existed in Greece by about 500 B.C.E. No law required that children go to school. There were not many schools for girls. The Greeks believed that girls could learn all they needed to know about running a household in the family home, so there was no need for them to go to school.

In Athens, at the age of seven years, boys from poorer homes went to school for about three to four years, to master basic **literacy.** Boys from better-off homes might go for up to ten years, starting at an earlier age and finishing at a later age. The richer children went with a trusted slave who made sure that they stuck to their studies and who reported back to their parents each day. Classes were usually small, composed of up to twelve children. Pupils who behaved badly were beaten with a stick.

What was taught at school?

There were three kinds of teachers. One kind taught reading, writing, arithmetic, and literature, which meant teaching long passages of poetry, particularly those by the poet Homer, by heart. Stories of the great heroes of the past were supposed to make boys want to grow up to be brave, too.

In this painting, a music teacher listens to his pupil play the pipes. The music teacher's lyre can be seen behind the boy's head.

This painted cup from about 500 B.C.E. shows a school scene from ancient Greece. We can see one student playing the lyre (left) and another reading aloud from a scroll (right).

The second kind of teacher was the sports coach, who supervised wrestling, gymnastics, and athletics. The third kind was a music master, who taught the **lyre,** singing, and the chanting of rhythmic poetry. Children from poorer homes may have missed out on this sort of education. The very rich might have a tutor at home but would probably still go to the local gymnasium for sports coaching and music lessons. This would enable them to take part in sports and writing contests that took place in every city.

Writing instruments and materials

The earliest Greek writings were scratched onto clay tablets or written on animal skins that had been scraped and stitched together as a continuous roll. By 600 B.C.E., the Greeks had begun to buy papyrus from Egypt. This was a kind of paper made from strips of pith from the reeds that grew along the river Nile. As these reeds would not grow in Greece, the Greeks were forced to go on importing the papyrus. Reed pens were used to write on it, with ink made from soot and vegetable gum. From 200 B.C.E. onward, the Greeks also began to use parchment, made from animal skins scraped as smooth as papyrus. As these materials were expensive, learners began to practice their letters in sand trays and then moved on to scratching them with a bronze or bone tool on wax tablets, which could be melted smooth and used again.

Reading, Writing, and Reciting

Literacy

In rich city-states such as Athens, most male **citizens** could probably read and write. There are no **statistics** that prove this, but there is plenty of evidence that suggests it. Each year Athenians could vote to send an unpopular citizen into **exile** for ten years. This was called ostracism because the names of candidates were scratched on a bit of broken pottery called an *ostrakon*. Any voter had to be able to write a name at least. Large numbers of **inscriptions** and graffiti have been found scratched on walls. These were often like modern advertisements or road signs, and they were designed to be read by as many people as possible. This suggests that many people could read. Even so, most foreign residents, women, and slaves were probably **illiterate.**

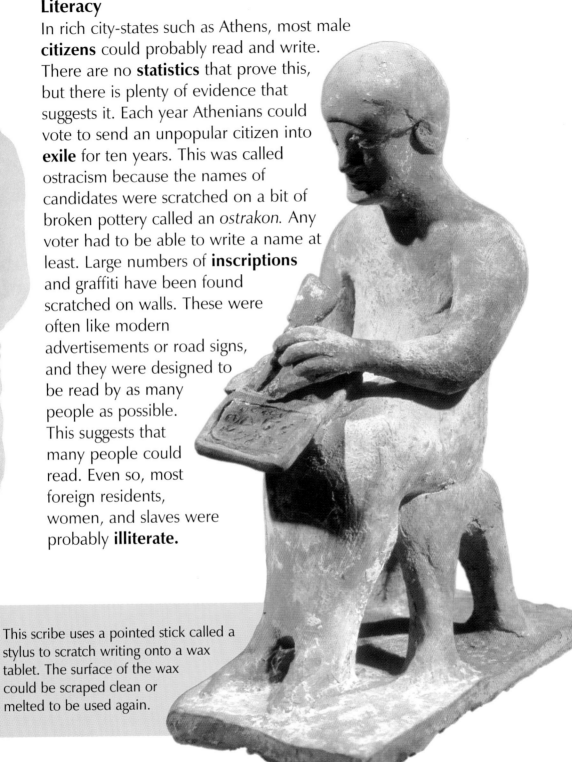

This scribe uses a pointed stick called a stylus to scratch writing onto a wax tablet. The surface of the wax could be scraped clean or melted to be used again.

Tall tales

Soon after the Greeks adopted an alphabet, in about 800 B.C.E., two ancient epic poems, the *Iliad* and the *Odyssey*, were written. These great adventure stories thrilled Greek children with tales of sea monsters and one-eyed giants. The Greeks thought that they were made up by a blind poet named Homer, who wrote them long ago. Some modern scholars think Homer's stories were actually those of several people, whose separate stories were mixed together. The poems were read aloud to a crowd rather than read silently by a single person, so people could enjoy them together. Although these poems had been written down, copies were written out by hand and were extremely expensive. Greek children learned most things by heart, from the teacher, rather than by reading books.

Speak up!

Greeks loved talking and admired people who could recite or make speeches well. Children learned poems and famous speeches by heart. The cleverest students then studied the art of public speaking, which Greeks called rhetoric. Rich young Athenians who wanted to go into politics paid a tutor called a Sophist to improve their skill at the art of argument. They learned to control nervousness, to improve their memory, to project their voice well, and to use jokes or clever sayings to get an audience on their side.

The alphabet

Widespread **literacy** resulted from Greek being written with an alphabet. Our word "alphabet" comes from the first two Greek letters: *alpha* and *beta*. The Romans then used the Greek alphabet to write **Latin.** Our alphabet is based on the Latin one. An alphabet has few symbols to learn. The Greek one varied over time from 24 to 26 symbols. Each symbol stands for a single sound that can be combined with others to make more sounds. Writing systems based on the representation of all the sounds in a language can have tens or even hundreds of symbols to learn. The writing system used in ancient Egypt is an example of such a system.

Math and Measurements

Greek thinkers were **pioneers** in mathematics. They also learned from the **Babylonians** and the Egyptians. The basic rules and terms of **geometry** were written down by Euclid, who lived around 300 B.C.E. His textbook was still being used as recently as one hundred years ago. Other Greek mathematicians used geometry to make advances in **astronomy** and to work out such problems as the **circumference** of the Earth. Despite these successes, the Greeks still used a very clumsy number system that was based on letters of the Greek alphabet written side by side. A four-figure number might be written with nine symbols.

This Greek coin, found at Samos, shows the famous Greek philosopher and mathematician Pythagoras. His ideas about mathematics are still being used today, more than 2,000 years after his death.

The calendar

Greek calendars were all based on the movements of the Moon but every city-state had its own system, with different names for the months and varying dates for the new year. Athenian months were named after festivals held during those months. Ordinary years had between 353 and 355 days, and leap years had an extra month and were made up of 383 to 385 days. Athenians also used two other calendars for deciding festival dates and dating government documents.

Arithmetic

Most Greek boys probably did not need to learn geometry, unless they wanted to become **architects.** Merchants' sons and even farmers' sons would have to know arithmetic to trade in the market. In many Greek households, wives kept the family accounts, so the learning of basic number skills may often have begun in the home.

Calculations were often done by use of a counting board or **abacus.** This was marked in vertical columns, with the biggest units on the right and numbers marked by use of pegs, counters, or pebbles. Merchants' sons would probably go with their fathers on their travels. They would have to learn about different types of coins, different systems of weights and measures, and foreign languages as well.

Telling the time

Greeks relied on sundials that were marked in twelve sections to show the length of daylight at a particular place. This meant that hours varied in length according to the season, because the length of daylight varied between summer and winter. At night or on cloudy days, a water clock could be used. This let water out at a constant rate, so that its level could be measured against a marked scale, which represented the passing hours.

Toys and Games

Few ancient Greek children's toys have survived, since most were easily broken or were destroyed, over time, by dampness or fire. Some have been found intact in tombs of young children. Others are illustrated in paintings on vases.

Family members made most toys. Children in rich families might have had toys that were made by skilled craftsmen. Babies were given clappers or rattles made from wood, clay pottery, or bone. Some had metal bells or loose pebbles inside. Dolls were made from cloth and wax and often had movable arms and legs. Dollhouses and the furniture inside them were made from wood. Models of farmyard animals and of pets were made from clay, wood, or bronze.

Metal hoops and wooden wheels, sometimes with bells attached, were used for bowling. Older children had spinning tops, swings, and many board games. There were also wooden hobby horses, small carts with wheels that were similar to modern go-carts, and **chariots** that had sails attached to make them go faster. Nuts were used as marbles. Knucklebones was a popular game. To play, a set of small bones had to be tossed up with one hand and caught on the back of the same hand.

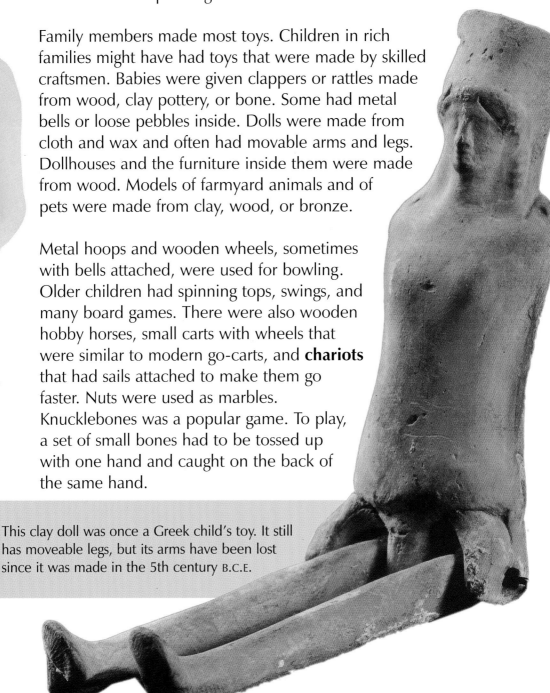

This clay doll was once a Greek child's toy. It still has moveable legs, but its arms have been lost since it was made in the 5th century B.C.E.

In the picture that decorates this vase, two small boys pull another boy in a two-wheeled cart .

Ball games

Ancient Greek children, as well as grown-ups, played many different ball games. One game that was played by both boys and girls involved players being carried on one another's backs and throwing the ball to, or past, one another. In another game, one player would throw a ball at a target, which another player tried to defend by catching or hitting the ball away. Vase paintings and carvings show many games. Some games look like football and hockey, but the precise rules are unknown.

Rubber and plastics were unknown to the ancient Greeks, but there were a number of ways to make a ball that would bounce. One way was to wrap the inflated bladder of a pig tightly inside a protective outer cover of animal skin or leather. A second way was to wind catgut or some other kind of animal **sinew** together like a ball of string and to cover this with skin or leather. A third way was to hold pieces of natural sponge together with string and to then wrap them in cloth. Sponge balls would not bounce nearly as well as the other kinds would, but they were easier to make. Younger children probably played with soft balls made of rags, feathers, or hair wrapped inside linen.

Sports

The ancient Greeks took sports very seriously as part of the education and military training of boys. Sports helped boys to become the sort of men whom Greeks admired: tough and competitive but also healthy and graceful. Sports also prepared boys for training as soldiers by encouraging strength, stamina, and bravery. Every town had a gymnasium with a running track and wrestling court.

Training and being good at sports was seen as a way of honoring the gods, and sports were a part of religious festivals. There were four games that drew competitors from the whole Greek world: the Olympic, Isthmian, Nemean, and Pythian games. The Greeks believed that the winners were favored by the gods who helped them to victory. Winners were honored with statues, poems, and prizes of cash or olive oil.

Each celebration of the games had separate competitions for boys of twelve to seventeen years of age, in running, wrestling, and boxing. Many fathers coached their sons. Former professional athletes became coaches when they retired. It was not unusual for sporting success to run in the family.

Racing
The Greeks raced horses and horse-drawn **chariots.** Jockeys rode without **stirrups,** which were unknown to the Greeks. Boys were

This carving shows Greek boys playing a game that looks like hockey.

These ruins are on the site where the ancient Olympic Games were held.

often chosen as jockeys because they were lighter than grown men. Chariot racing was the highest rated of all sports and one of the most dangerous. Competitors followed an oval course, about 2,000 feet (about 600 meters) long, and rounded a post at either end. With no barrier between chariots going in opposite directions, crashes were frequent. On one occasion, among 41 starters, only the winner finished. Because chariots and horses were expensive, racing was only for the wealthy. The prize for winning went to the chariot's owner, not the driver who had risked his life.

Athletics

Athletic contests included sprinting, long-distance running, long jump, and discus or javelin throwing. The only contests in which girls could, separately, compete were sprints. Girls wore a **tunic,** unless they were Spartans, who ran naked. Spartan girls were encouraged to play rough sports to toughen themselves up for childbirth.

Combat sports

No equipment was needed, so anyone could wrestle, although there were separate competitions for boys. As there were no weight classes, heavier, stronger people had an advantage. Punching was banned, but breaking fingers was allowed. Wrestlers fought naked but were coated in olive oil. Boxing was less popular, except in Sparta, and was even more brutal. Boxers' fists were bound with leather. There were no rounds, and fights went on until one fighter gave up or was knocked out.

Sickness and Health

Healthy living

The ancient Greeks knew that a varied diet, fresh air, sleep, and exercise were good for health. Yet even healthy people usually died by the age of 50 years. Children, especially, died from **infectious** diseases common in summer. The biggest killers were **malaria** and, in crowded towns, **tuberculosis.** Younger children died from **dysentery,** caused by poor hygiene and dirty water.

The Greeks were usually vague about population figures, except when describing the fighting force of a *polis.* Women, slaves, foreigners, and children would generally be ignored, so it is difficult to find accurate information about health. Skeletons provide basic evidence about ages at and causes of death. **Excavations** of cemeteries suggest that the death rate in the first year after birth was high. Probably about one of every three children died before he or she was two years old.

These statues show two girls playing Knucklebones. Girls of this age were lucky to have survived early childhood, but they died young by today's standards.

If a child managed to survive to the age of three years, then it would probably reach adulthood, although snake and insect bites, as well as serious burns, cuts, or falls, could also lead to an early death.

Helpers and healers

Most children relied on their family to treat them with traditional medicines based on herbs and natural products such as olive oil, vinegar, honey, or garlic. Milk, not part of a regular diet, was often used as a medicine. Medical help was given by sellers of drugs, herbs or charms, and by midwives and gymnastic trainers as well as doctors.

Balance for health

The ancient Greeks believed that four substances, or humors, controlled the body and that when these were unbalanced illness resulted. Bleeding, sweating, and vomiting were thought to restore the balance. Medical **theory,** which had some **scientific** ideas, was mixed with belief in the healing powers of prayers, spells, and dreams. The ancient Greeks knew nothing useful about highly infectious diseases, such as **plague.** Young children were most vulnerable to these diseases because they were not strong enough to survive them.

Doctors

No law required doctors to be qualified, so anyone could call himself a doctor. Doctors ranked with skilled workers, such as **architects.** Even the most famous Greek doctor ever, Hippocrates, admitted that more than half his patients died. He warned his students that patients "won't take medicine they do not like ... and sometimes die as a result ... and the doctor gets the blame." Doctors knew how to set bones, **amputate** limbs, and clean and bind up cuts. Surgery was a last resort, because patients usually died from the shock of the pain, loss of blood, or infection afterward.

Beliefs and Behavior

Gods

The ancient Greeks believed in many gods and thought that these gods lived on Mount Olympus in northern Greece. Gods had to be pleased with food and gifts, animal **sacrifices,** and festivals. They were like humans, who fell in love, got married, had children, and quarreled. Gods also had superhuman powers, such as invisibility or the ability to turn into animals or to foretell the future. Each god had special interests. Artemis, goddess of hunting, wild animals, and wild places, was also goddess of the Moon and childbirth. Her twin brother, Apollo, was god of the Sun, shepherds, music, and medicine.

Religious Ceremonies

Girls played an important part in many religious **ceremonies.** The ancient Greeks believed that contact with death or disease polluted a person. Such pollution made them unfit to take part in religious ceremonies until they had been purified by washing, making a **sacrifice,** or simply waiting out the passage of time.

The young boy in this carving is having water poured over him as part of a religious ceremony.

A girl whose parents were still living—so she was not polluted by death—was believed to be most suitable for helping priests perform **rituals.** This might involve washing the statue of a god, carrying olive branches in processions to a **temple,** or grinding corn to make special cakes as offerings for the gods. Girls taking part in these rituals often came from a few wealthy families. Boys went with their fathers to major religious occasions to learn what to do when they grew up, but they had to wait until they were old enough for military training before they had their own important part to play.

Goodness

The ancient Greeks were very interested in what it meant to be good and spent much time arguing and thinking about the question. Their ideas of goodness had little to do with religion. Gods themselves were believed to behave spitefully or wickedly. A person did not behave well to please the gods but for the sake of his reputation and the honor of his family, *phratry,* and *polis.*

Learning these values would have been an important part of a child's upbringing. A good man was brave, loyal, and clever. Kindness, except for generosity to friends and strangers, was not that important. Showing off at sports, music, or public speaking was fine, providing that the show-off had real talent. Making a fool of oneself brought shame not only to a person but also to that person's family.

Spartan values

Some of the ideas that ancient Greek children would have learned seem strange to us now. Spartans thought that lying, cheating, and stealing were useful skills, especially in times of war. Only cowardice was unforgivable. Greeks in most city-states believed that a good woman was obedient, hard-working, silent, devoted to her husband, and bore many children.

Holidays and Festivals

Ancient Greek festivals were held to honor the gods. They were holidays in the sense that regular work stopped, except for essential tasks such as fetching water and feeding animals. Village children, wearing their best clothes, would come from the countryside with their families to take part in the celebrations.

Anthesteria

Each spring a festival called *Anthesteria* was held, to honor Dionysus, the god of wine, and to mark the first stage in the passage toward manhood of children, who, at three years of age, were no longer babies. With flowers in their hair, they went to a **temple** to take their first sips of wine from a small clay jug that was kept as a souvenir.

Small wine jugs were given to boys at the *Anthesteria* festival, when they reached their third birthday.

Time off

The festival calendar followed the farmer's year, which began in July. Major celebrations marked the plowing and sowing of the fields and, later, the gathering of the crops. These were supposed to make sure that there would be a good harvest and plenty to eat throughout the year. Every *polis* also held a big festival to honor its **guardian** god or goddess, whom the citizens of the *poleis* believed would protect the *polis* and its people. In addition to major occasions organized by the *polis*, there were also many local celebrations organized by each village and *phratry*. Adding in these minor events means that almost half the days in the year were marked by some sort of celebration, although not everybody would stop working for all of them. Probably about 60 festival days a year could be thought of as holidays in something like the modern sense.

Festivals usually followed the same general order: a procession to a temple, the **sacrifice** of expensive animals (such as bulls), contests, and a feast at the end. Women, foreigners, slaves, and children could usually join in processions, although priests and older men normally went first. Sacrifices were solemn and included prayers. Girls were often chosen to carry the instruments that were used for sacrifice. Part of the sacrificed animal was left for the god, but most was set aside for the feast. Then came plays, sports such as races or wrestling, the reciting of poetry, and competitions between choirs or musicians. There were separate contests for adults and children. Although there was a banquet, drinking, and dancing, festivals were also serious. Children learned about the gods who governed their lives and about the heroes they should admire.

Growing Up

For some boys, putting on their swords and helmets and beginning work as a soldier meant the end of their childhood.

Boys

Teenage boys, who had been shown to members of their father's **phratry** when they were babies, were introduced again on the last day of a three-day autumn festival called *Apaturia*. At eighteen years of age, boys in Athens and a number of other city-states began two years of military service. The first year was spent training in **barracks;** the second year was spent guarding the borders of the **polis.** When they were 30 years of age, they could begin to take part in government and could sit on juries.

Girls

Girls became women when they reached **puberty** and their bodies changed so that they could have babies of their own. They would go to a shrine or **temple** dedicated to the goddess Artemis and leave their favorite dolls and toys at the altar to show that their childhood was over. Most of the time, this happened just before a girl got married.

Marriage

Girls married in their early teens. The husband was often twice their age or more. No law required that the girl agree to the marriage, and there was no need for a priest to conduct the **ceremony.** The law usually required that both husband and wife should be **citizens** of a *polis* if their children were to be recognized as citizens of that *polis*. Husbands usually got a **dowry** of cash or land, but this was a matter of custom, not law.

Weddings

The wedding ceremony began with baths in water that had been carried by children from a **sacred** spring or fountain. The bride and groom then dressed in their finest clothes for a feast at the house of the bride's father. During the feast, the bride took off her veil to show herself to her husband, and he gave her gifts. A boy whose parents were both still alive carried around a basket of bread as a sign of good luck. In the evening, the whole party went in a procession, with musicians and well-wishers, to the husband's house. There the newlyweds were led to the **hearth** and showered with nuts and sweets. A bride was only recognized as truly being a member of her new family, however, after she had her first baby. This shows how important children were, both to the Greek family and in the role of being a wife.

This vase shows the great trouble taken to prepare a bride for her wedding.

How Do We Know?

Lost evidence

Most of what the ancient Greeks made is lost forever. We know homes had wooden couches. However, not one such couch has survived, although some bronze decorative couch fittings have. Items made of the most common materials—wood, wax, clay, cloth, bone, and leather—were broken, burned, or have rotted away. The same is true of papyrus or parchment documents.

Athens, Athens, Athens,...

More, both written and crafted, has survived from rich, powerful Athens than from anywhere else in the ancient Greek world. The survival of these materials, however, can distort our view of the past. In the same way, it would be very difficult to study the history of North America if we only had evidence of what happened in major cities such as Toronto or New York.

Marble carvings such as this one, from the Parthenon in Athens, have survived over the centuries and give archaeologists vital clues about the past. Materials such as wood or cloth have not survived.

These columns in the shape of young women are called caryatids. They are found at many temples in Greece.

Tombs, teeth, and treasures

Despite these problems, we do have some hard evidence. Children's tombs often contain favorite dolls, toys, and feeding bottles. They also have **inscriptions** that show how sad parents were that their child had died. Children's skeletons sometimes show signs of accidents or illness. Modern technology also enables **archaeologists** to use tooth enamel to find out from adult skeletons if they were ill or underfed as children.

The ancient Greeks made painted vases showing scenes from everyday life. These vases are great treasures not only because they are rare and beautiful but also because they record a past that would otherwise remain lost and unknown. The vase paintings you have seen in this book tell us a lot about ancient Greek children. There is still much that we do not know about growing up in ancient Greece. We can see that life for Greek children, with its toys, games, and schoolwork, was similar in some ways to the way that we live now. Many parts of our lives, from school to government, would be very different without the example of ancient Greece.

Timeline

All the following dates are B.C.E.:

c. 3000–c. 1450	Greece is controlled by Minoan kings from Crete.
c. 1600–c. 1100	Greek-speaking Mycenaeans rule separate kingdoms in mainland Greece.
c. 1100–c. 800	Greece goes through a period of wars and migration.
c. 800–c. 700	Homer's *Iliad* and *Odyssey* were probably written; Greece is made up of small city-states that are ruled by separate kings or noble families.
c. 750–c. 550	Greeks set up colonies in lands around the Mediterranean Sea.
c. 500	Some city-states become democracies; of these, Athens is the most powerful.
c. 490–479	The main period of **Persian** invasions of Greece occurs.
431–404	The **Peloponnesian** War, between Greek city-states, ends with Sparta eclipsing Athens as the most powerful state in mainland Greece.
378–371	Sparta is eclipsed by a new power, Thebes.
336–323	Greece is ruled by Alexander the Great of Macedon after his invasion and conquest.
146	Greece becomes part of the Roman Empire.

More Books to Read

Barron's Educational Editors. *Greek Life.* Hauppage, N.Y.: Barron's
    Educational Services, Inc., 1998.

Bartole, Mira, and Christine Ronan. *Ancient Greece.* Parsippany, N.J.:
    Pearson Learning, 1995.

Clare, John D., ed., *Ancient Greece.* New York: Harcourt Children's
    Books, 1994.

Day, Nancy. *Your Travel Guide to Ancient Greece.* Minneapolis: Lerner
    Publishing Group, 2000. An older reader can help you with this book.

Ganeri, Anita. *Ancient Greeks.* Danbury, Conn.: Franklin Watts, 1993.

Malam, John. *A Greek Town.* Danbury, Conn.: Franklin Watts, 1999.

Nardo, Don. *Life in Ancient Greece.* Farmington Hills, Mich.: The Gale
    Group, 1996. An older reader can help you with this book.

Pearson, Anne. *Ancient Greece.* New York: Dorling-Kindersley Publishers,
    Inc., 2000.

Rees, Rosemary. *The Ancient Greeks.* Chicago: Heinemann Library, 1997.

Glossary

abacus wooden frame with rows of beads on wires, used for counting

ammunition stones, arrows, or other objects to fire from weapons

amputate to cut off part of the body

archaeologist person who studies buildings and objects from the past to discover how people lived

archery art of using a bow and arrows

architect person who designs buildings

astronomy study of the stars and planets

Babylonia ancient civilization in what is now Iraq

barracks building or buildings in which soldiers live apart from other people

brazier metal container for holding lighted coals

catapult machine for firing stones or arrows

cavalry soldiers who fight on horseback

ceremony ritual performed to mark an occasion such as a birthday or a wedding

chariot two-wheeled cart used for warfare

circumference the distance around something

citizen person with the right to take part in politics, in particular, by voting

civilization distinct way of life that is common to a particular group of people

courtyard enclosed area surrounded by high walls

dedicated made especially for, or given to

democracy method of government by which citizens can elect their own rulers

dowry marriage gift from the brides family, consisting of money, land, or goods

drill exercise to train soldiers to act as a team and follow orders

dysentery stomach infection that causes the sufferer to go to the toilet repeatedly

excavation digging in search of buried items from the past

exile to ban, or send away, from one's own country

flax plant whose fibers are made into linen

fodder food for animals

frieze carved horizontal band of sculpture that runs around a building

geometry branch of mathematics concerned with shapes, surfaces, and solids

grazing land area with grass or plants for animals to eat

guardian person who looks after or protects

hearth place for a fire

historian person who uses written documents to find out what happened in the past

illiterate unable to read or write

infantry soldiers who fight on foot

infectious can be caught from another person

inherit to get something from a person who has died

inscription writing carved into a surface, such as a monument or a coin

Latin language of ancient Rome

literacy ability to read and write

lyre stringed musical instrument

malaria infectious disease spread by mosquitoes

martyr someone who dies for his or her religious beliefs

mess group of soldiers who share meals

myth ancient story about a god or hero

oikos Greek household

Peloponnese southern region of mainland Greece

philosopher person interested in thoughts and theories, from the Greek words meaning lover of knowledge

phratry (more than one are called *phratrai*) group of clans that was a subdivision of a *phyla*. Each individual *phratry* was supposed to come from a shared ancestor.

phyla (more than one are called *phylae*) tribe to which households belonged

physician doctor

pioneer person who goes somewhere or does something first

plague disease spread by fleas or other carriers, often resulting in death

polis (more than one are called *poleis*) Greek city-state

protein food element vital to health

puberty stage of life when the male or female body becomes capable of producing or bearing children, respectively

ritual ordered actions or gestures that are performed for the purpose of worship

sacred holy or concerned with the gods

sacrifice a creature, usually an animal, killed and dedicated to the gods

scientific based on ideas proved by tests and experiments

sinew strand on muscle that attaches it to bone

statistics systematic collection of figures for measurement and comparison

stirrup metal ring, hung from a saddle, in which a rider puts his or her foot

temple building for religious purposes

theory idea to explain something

tuberculosis infectious disease of the lungs

tunic sleeveless garment for the body, often gathered at the waist

weave to intertwine fibers horizontally and vertically to make cloth

wreath circle of entwined branches

Index